SPOTLIGHT ON
AN EQUITABLE WORLD

EXPLORING IDENTITIES

Mary Ratzer

ROSEN
PUBLISHING

Published in 2025 by The Rosen Publishing Group, Inc.
2544 Clinton Street, Buffalo, NY 14224

First Edition

Editor: Greg Roza
Book Design: Michael Flynn

Photo Credits: Cover simona pilolla 2/Shutterstock.com; cover, p. 3 (hands) Dedraw Studio/Shutterstock.com; (series Earth icon) v4ndhira/Shutterstock.com; p. 5 Maya Kruchankova/Shutterstock.com; p. 6 airdone/Shutterstock.com; p. 7 Creativa Images/Shutterstock.com; p. 9 digitalskillet/Shutterstock.com; p. 10 https://commons.wikimedia.org/wiki/File:Logo_HGP.jpg/Shutterstock.com; p. 11 YAKOBCHUK VIACHESLAV/Shutterstock.com; pp. 13, 18 PeopleImages.com - Yuri A/Shutterstock.com; p. 14 Monkey Business Images/Shutterstock.com; p. 15 Alena Ozerova/Shutterstock.com; p. 17 LightField Studios/Shutterstock.com; p. 19 Prostock-studio/shutterstock.com; p. 21 Daniel Chetroni/Shutterstock.com; p. 22 Johnny Silvercloud/Shutterstock.com; p. 23 courtesy of the Library of Congress; p. 25 Michele Vacchiano/Shutterstock.com; p. 26 Steve Sanchez Photos/Shutterstock.com; p. 27 https://commons.wikimedia.org/wiki/File:Patrick_Mahomes_(51614638067)_(cropped).jpg; p. 29 Amparo Garcia/Shutterstock.com.

Cataloging-in-Publication Data

Names: Ratzer, Mary Boyd.
Title: Exploring identities / Mary Ratzer.
Description: Buffalo, NY : Rosen Young Adult, 2025. | Series: Spotlight on an equitable world | Includes glossary and index.
Identifiers: ISBN 9781499477399 (pbk.) | ISBN 9781499477252 (library bound) | ISBN 9781499476972 (ebook)
Subjects: LCSH: Self-perception--Juvenile literature. | Self-consciousness (Awareness)--Juvenile literature. | Identity (Psychology) in adolescence--Juvenile literature.
Classification: LCC BF697.5.S43 R38 2025 | DDC 158.1--dc23

Manufactured in the United States of America

CONTENTS

Chapter One

PAST, PRESENT, AND FUTURE YOU

Self-awareness is the ability to understand your own emotions, thoughts, and values. It's an important life skill. Paying attention to emotions, thoughts, and values lets you understand your words, choices, and actions. The invisible parts of your identity are developing and make you who you are. Words, actions, and behavior are part of what others see of your identity. Can you think of a moment when this happened?

Your identity changes over time. In some ways you are a different person every day. A part of your brain holds a strong sense of your identity, or your sense of self. Your personal and social identity gets very special treatment in your brain. The memories that are about you and your experiences are stronger and different from memories about general facts. They are set apart and easy to access. You are a work in progress and so is your identity. You can visualize the person you will be in the future shaped by your values and goals.

Memories are the glue that bring your past and present selves together. You can also imagine the future self you are becoming. Your brain is equipped to tell your story and hold onto your ever-developing identity. The fact that you can think about your past, present, and future self gives you a look inside the person you are. Looking at the past, you might reflect on a quality that you changed for the better. Your present identity is being affected by your relationships and growing self-awareness.

Your identity is how you see yourself, but it's also shaped by how others see you.

Chapter Two

IDENTITY UNDER CONSTRUCTION

How teens view themselves shifts quickly as they think about big questions such as: *Who am I? Who is my best self? How do I see myself? How do others see me? Should I change myself to fit in?* Young people in this stage of development have a strong need to be accepted by peers, bond with friends, and win the rewards of popularity. They try on aspects of identity to belong. On the path to becoming themselves, they look through the lenses of peers, parents, and other respected adults.

The building blocks of identity include experiences that open pathways to new perspectives. Developing new strengths and talents shapes self-awareness. Success and positive relationships support the ability to form alliances and cooperate with others. These alliances confirm values important to a person's identity. Desirable traits that

"Who am I?" is a simple question, but one that may be difficult to answer. How would you answer this question?

are key to healthy connections become stronger. Negative experiences, such as being isolated or rejected by peers, are painful and stressful. New identities involve risks such as insecurity, challenging choices, and growing independence.

Learning the skills of understanding feedback and empathy is a pathway to becoming your best self. By looking closely at your values and doing the right thing, you build a foundation for actions and decisions. When mature, a person may finally shape an identity that answers the question: *Who am I?* That may not happen until the age of 24 or 25. So identity is a work in progress that requires awareness, experiences, openness to differences, positive relationships, and reflection.

Chapter Three

IDENTITY THROUGH RESPECTFUL EYES

For some teens, middle school and high school come with a struggle to keep a positive self-image. Identity is a work in progress. Feedback, self-doubt, mean speech, and the pressure to fit in create insecurity and stress. Teachers in Roseville High School in Detroit decided to write letters to students who inspire them. Handwritten notes of gratitude from teachers uplifted kids who overcame struggles, shared good will, proved their resilience, or made their world a better place. The letters were shared one-on-one, shining a positive light on recipients.

Self-image can be changed by the perceptions of others. This change can be positive. Respectful eyes observe what goes unnoticed to others. A caring friend, teacher, or parent can a shine light on an unrecognized aspect of character or identity. A national campaign called #WHYYOUMATTER focuses on kids expressing their own sense of why they matter. Students write a statement about why they matter, photograph it, and share it with teachers and friends. The pictures are a daily reminder of personal worth. At the end of the year teachers write a personal note on the back of each picture and share their reasons why students matter to them.

One significant and caring adult has the power to overcome isolation and insecurity that harms a student's sense of self. Mentors, coaches, club advisers, grandparents, and friends can be a mirror for self-images that have endured negative feedback or mean speech. The potential to give self-worth back to someone because of respect is a powerful force for the good.

You never know who will become a mentor to you and influence you in a positive way. Mentors can be family members, bosses, religious leaders, coaches, and more.

Chapter Four

THE HUMAN FAMILY

Like a family of 8 billion people, all humans on Earth are related, connected, and almost identical. The Human Genome Project was a historic scientific research effort. Starting over 30 years ago, it mapped the complex parts of our cells that make us unique human beings. We inherit most of our makeup as a human from our family. Sometimes we look just like our grandfather or have brown eyes just like our mom. We could be tall like our dad or musical like our sister.

There is a truly amazing discovery from this project. We are all so different: how we look, our talents, our voices, our personalities, and so much more. But in our cells, almost 100 percent of the stuff that makes us part of the human species is the same! All our many differences only add up to one tiny bit of us. The human species is 99.9% identical. We are one big human family.

The Human Genome Project was an international scientific effort to map and sequence all of the genes in human DNA, also called the "human genome."

Researchers have explored many things that are similar about humans, even though they speak different languages and live thousands of miles apart. These similarities are evidence that, in many ways, we all have the same needs, wants, and dreams. All humans have some basic emotions such as fear, anger, enjoyment, surprise, and sadness. Infant care, dance, love, and mourning have many similarities. Cultures share many of the same problems and solve them in the same way. All countries have economies to provide goods, ways of supporting marriage and family, education for children, laws, communication, and the arts.

Chapter Five

MULTIPLE IDENTITIES

Your school, classes, teams, clubs, and community are each a small universe of identities. In every seat and hallway in your school is a person with a unique and complex social identity. Some of the many pieces that make up someone's identity are visible, and some are not. Race, ethnicity, gender, sexual orientation, economic class status, religion, ability, citizenship, nation of origin, and age are all part of your identity. You can represent your multiple identities in a graphic or identity wheel. Ask your parents or grandparents questions to fill in the blanks.

By engaging with friends and classmates, you begin to recognize what makes each of them individuals as well as part of a culture and community. Social awareness is always growing with experiences and relationships. You are continually learning about the differences and similarities between people who are part of your real world. Growing in a community with multiple identities leads to skills related to relationships, collaboration, and multiple perspectives.

The United States is becoming more and more diverse. The future of our society depends on the assets of diversity. Varied backgrounds and experiences contribute valued talents and strengths. A diverse workforce is a success story for business and organizations. Diversity encourages comfort in sharing. Brainstorming and problem-solving benefit from new ideas and diverse perspectives.

In the real world of business, sports, or public service, the best results come from diverse teams who collaborate. Skills, perspectives, and abilities of diverse team members solve community problems. Differences make teams stronger.

Attending college for the first time can be a whole new experience for many. It's often a chance to meet new people from differnt backgrounds and to share your own culture.

Chapter Six

SOCIAL IDENTITY

A baby is born with connections to social groups that will shape their identity. Families often celebrate and carefully select a name for their new member. Sometimes the name reflects cultural or ethnic ties, family history, and/or strong links to social identity. Perhaps a religious ritual welcomes this baby into that community. Maybe this child will learn to speak two languages because the family came to the United States from another country. Belonging to a family means belonging to a culture. Belonging to a family means having a history, a way to celebrate, special foods, customs, beliefs, and deep connections with people and places.

Curiosity about your identity can start a quest for understanding and appreciation. As you grow older, you see how your identity is connected to many groups by birth or choice. You may have connections to explore that you never knew existed. Thinking about questions you might have leads to investigating, conversations, photographs, family treasures, music, and more.

Writing in a journal frequently will help you explore yourself and make sense of the world around you.

Starting a journal can lead to a deeper understanding of your social identity. Start with questions that give you a purpose for investigating and growing in self-awareness:

- **What parts of your social identity do you think about the most? Why?**
- **What parts of your social identity do you not think about very often?**
- **What parts of your social identity would you like to know more about?**
- **Which aspects of your social identity are the strongest influences on you?**
- **What aspects of your social identity do others see?**

Chapter Seven

CLUBS, TEAMS, AFTER-SCHOOL ACTIVITIES

Belonging to groups supports a developing identity. Discovering character traits, talents, and strengths comes with new experiences. These experiences have proven power. Working closely with others is a pathway to develop a positive sense of self and values. Belonging to teams and clubs is a way to explore possibilities. Learning life skills, developing character, and thriving because of positive relationships is just the beginning.

Belonging teaches you responsibility, confidence, problem solving, and a sense of personal agency. Teamwork leads to learning how you can be an ally, or even a leader. Seeing new perspectives and engaging with role models builds your character. Communication, relationships, and connections are life-long assets.

Reaching out to people in need can be the path to a sense of belonging. For example, this is a letter to a student from a teacher advising a service-based club:

> Two years ago, I met you when you came to our club meeting with a friend who already belonged. I have seen so many positive results of our efforts here and in the community. But I could tell you were unsure.
>
> You stayed and made many new friends, including me. We have all learned about you and from you. I want you to know you have my respect and the gratitude of so many members who have depended on you. You have proven to be someone that all of us trust as we work together. You have proven that your confidence and abilities make you a willing leader. I thank you for being a strong, creative, and caring person. We are all so glad you stayed!

Adult club leaders can be a great source of advice and encouragement for teens. They want to see you succeed!

Chapter Eight

SOCIAL MEDIA AND IDENTITY

Throughout adolescence, you are figuring out who you are. Your identity is still taking shape. Being a part of identity-safe environments means that self-esteem and personal well-being are supported. Social media may not be an identity-safe environment for young people who have a negative self-image, mental health challenges, or are lonely.

Making the decision to be on social media encourages you to compare yourself with others. People share their lives on social media sites such as Instagram to get the most likes and followers. What you see is often a false picture of people. Not everything that your peers share online is real. Peers must compare who they really are with their social media self. They can still make you feel unhappy if you believe you fall short of their qualities and appeal. Making comparisons to

Endlessly scrolling through social media sites can lead to depression, anxiety, and apathy. It's best to unplug and seek healthier activities.

others on social media could give you poor self-esteem. Becoming a target of bullies or online groups puts you at risk of having negative feelings and thoughts about who you are.

Social media has a strong influence on the mental health of middle schoolers and teens. One in four consider it a negative experience. TikTok, Instagram, and Snapchat are designed to get you plugged in and keep you there. Engaging with social media before the age of 14 has been proven to be harmful to mental health, self-image, and relationships. Social media can cause depression and anxiety to increase with the time spent scrolling. Average daily contact with social media by people your age is 5 to 6 hours, with some spending up to 9 hours online.

Chapter Nine

CAUTION: BIAS ALERT

Bias is a part of media history. Identity is affected by how people see people like themselves in movies, TV shows, and social media. The way media portrays members of racial or ethnic groups can affect identity in a negative way. Some social media sites show videos of violence among teens and show teen arrests. Popular choices for media consumers, this kind of video plays over and over. Formulas called algorithms determine what users see and how they see it on social media. Regardless of the impact on the identity of young viewers, bias is built into these formulas.

Bias in media causes long-term psychological impacts on teenagers, many of whom spend many hours a day online. Adolescents can experience a loss of self-esteem regarding their identity. A research study found that 95 percent of teens have access to a smartphone. Hispanic teens, in particular, spend more time online than their white peers, according to the same study. Bias impacts an adolescent audience with serious consequences.

TikTok filters what young people see and hear. One effect of this filtering is encouraging adolescents to find content that matches their own ethnicity, race, or gender expression. As empathy tends to drop off in adolescence, young people avoid the differences they need to experience. Their real world is becoming more and more diverse. TikTok and other media options are aware of this problem. It's important to understand that adolescent brain development makes them more likely to be affected negatively by bias in social media.

With so many social media platforms to choose from, it can be hard to break away from your smartphone or computer.

Chapter Ten

IDENTITY, BIAS, AND INJUSTICE

History holds many lessons about identity and injustice. Over the centuries, certain groups have been targets of hateful actions and words. Black people, Native Americans, and many immigrant groups have endured historic injustices. Today, a clear connection continues between bias, injustice, and identity. But there have been allies and role models who fought against such hate. Taking responsibility to do the right thing and think of others, individuals act against hate. Any active citizen can make the decision to be a part of the solution to this problem.

Negative beliefs about group identity cause widespread harm. Bias and stereotyping deny groups and individuals their human dignity and fairness. Hateful speech, discrimination in housing and employment, blocked access to quality education, and acts of violence happen every day.

Many people have stood up for civil rights in U.S. history, and many of them have paid a terrible price for their action. Martin Luther King Jr. was an outspoken civil rights leader in the 1960s. Unfortunately, he was shot and killed for his beliefs on April 4, 1968.

Many years of effort and millions of voices put laws in place to protect the rights of those impacted by discrimination and violence. The Civil Rights Act of 1965, the Equal Employment Opportunity Commission, and U.S. anti-discrimination laws are enforced by the U.S. Department of Justice. Violent actions and discrimination are crimes. Victims have protection under the law. By 2040, ethnic groups that are currently in the minority will be the majority. Every fair-minded and caring person is responsible for respecting differences and understanding other cultures.

Chapter Eleven

IN-GROUPS AND OUT-GROUPS

Human ancestors lived in small groups that often competed with others to survive. Due to threats of harm from competitors, groups often developed negative beliefs about other groups. Human brains are wired to set up categories for people and see others as part of groups. The members of in-groups have important similarities. The out-group members have important differences. Members of each group can develop biased attitudes about the other. Just being a member of an in-group boosts self-esteem because that group identifies with positive qualities.

Today, young children favor in-groups and people like themselves. Children prefer to play with the same gender and the same race as themselves by age 3. Many cultures of the world favor certain in-groups. Cultures believe that in-group members are more positive, resulting in bias and barriers to relationships.

About 150 years ago, immigrants to America used in-group/out-group categories for protection and support. Neighborhoods in cities were often home to one ethnic group. Irish, Italian, and German people stuck together. Celebrations of in-group identity still have a part in some people's lives, such as a St. Patrick's Day parade. Families may have reacted negatively to a member connecting with someone in an out-group.

The lines of difference have disappeared over time, while new lines take shape. Many in-groups can be diverse but still have one special quality that is favored and unites them. Creating connections between groups depends on fair thinking and fair action.

Many immigrants chose to settle in New York City throughout the 1800s, and they often created isolated communities. Even today, parts of the city have names such as Chinatown and Little Italy.

Chapter Twelve

ROLE MODELS

Role models show young people how to view their world through a positive lens. They inspire young people to make responsible decisions that affect their attitudes and behavior. Their sense of responsibility to fight hate and think of others guides young people to become that kind of person. The Federal Bureau of Investigation (FBI) says hate crimes against certain groups, including Asian Americans, Jews, and LGBTQIA+ individuals, rose to more than 11,000 events in 2022.

One well-known role model is the quarterback for the Kansas City Chiefs, Patrick Mahomes. This star player has called on his fellow National Football League (NFL) players to be role models as racial injustice impacts so many. Although the NFL hasn't always been an ally for racial justice in the past, players like Mahomes have worked to change that. As a well-respected athlete in the public eye, Mahomes is using his voice for justice: "We need to come together as players and… be the role models."

Mahomes's leadership skill is inspirational and undeniable. He has led the Kansas City Chiefs to three Super Bowl victories, and has won the Super Bowl most-valuable player award three times.

Mahomes's words give you an insight to his values and goals: "I grew up in a locker room where people from every race, every background, and every community come together and become brothers to accomplish a single goal. I hope our country can learn from the injustices we have witnessed to become more like the locker room where everyone is accepted. We all need to treat each other like brothers and sisters and become something better."

Chapter Thirteen

SELF-RESPECT

The journey to becoming a person who is secure in who they are is not an easy one. Self-respect is earned through your own choices, actions, and values. There is no straight line that gets you there. Although empathy and compassion are clearly ideals to pursue, differences present challenges. Relationships can build self-respect or break it down. Feedback can be sincere, kind, and welcome. Or it can be mean and destructive. Being a part of a targeted group can be so difficult. Ask yourself: *Can I stand up to bullies? Can I be an ally?*

One teacher or one family member who knows you and values you can be all you need. An invitation to be included and getting likes on your selfie photo motivate your actions. Learning from mistakes can bring positive change. Weighing your own self-image against how others see you is a challenge to say the least.

Getting in touch with your identity requires thoughtful reflection. This can lead you to recognize the positive and negative aspects of your self-image. Recognizing the factors and influences that shape your self-image form a foundation for a self-portrait. Drawing, graphical representations, poetry, music, a letter to a friend or parent, or another creative expression could capture the person you are. Self-respect starts with the conviction that you know who you are and you like who you are. With that starting point, you can move forward with confidence. Self-respect and self-knowledge give you freedom to become what you want to be.

Creativity and self-expression can help you learn about your own identity and share it with others around you.

Chapter Fourteen

BE BRAVE

Exploring identities takes courage. A brave person makes connections across differences and welcomes diversity. Sharing your culture or expressing your beliefs takes you out of safe invisibility. Valuing your ethnicity prompts you to share. Welcoming a new classmate with just a smile or an introduction moves you out of your comfort zone. Deciding not to go along with your peers when they bully someone risks your relationships with them.

Many adolescents and middle school students bravely work for fairness. They see a problem and they take action. Because of their values and beliefs, they find the courage to act. Young people are being brave and finding ways to shine light on problems and demand solutions. Greta Thunberg sailed across the Atlantic Ocean for 15 days in her global quest for climate justice to attend the U.N. Climate Action Summit in 2019. Standing up against book challenges, teens and middle schoolers are presenting at board of education meetings in many communities. Sixteen kids in Montana are suing their state for environmental quality and going to court. Young activists were a part of the Civil Rights Movement of the 1960s, going to jail as 12-year-olds. School shootings turned Marjory Stoneman Douglas High School students in Florida into national leaders and spokespersons for safe schools.

Being brave means caring deeply enough about others that you don't wait for someone else to act. You don't keep quiet. You don't look away. You act on empathy, a sense of fairness, your values, and character bravely.

GLOSSARY

algorithm: A step-by-step procedure for solving a problem or accomplishing some end.

alliance: A union between persons, families, or parties.

collaboration: An instance when people work together toward a common goal.

condemn: To declare to be wrong.

conviction: A strong belief.

discrimination: The treating of some people better than others without any fair or proper reason.

DNA: The material in the body that create chromosomes, which carry genetic information. Short for deoxyribonucleic acid.

empathy: The ability to understand another person's feelings, experiences, and emotions.

evidence: Something that shows that something else is true.

insecurity: Lack of a reliable means of meeting one's basic needs.

isolate: Set apart from others.

mentor: To teach, give guidance, or give advice to someone, especially a less experienced person.

personal agency: A sense of self, including goals and interests.

resilience: The ability to recover from or adjust to misfortune or change.

stereotype: An unfair and often untrue belief about someone or a group of people.

INDEX